*It is in silence that God
is known, and through
mysteries that He
declares Himself.*
Robert Hugh Benson

101 ways to give your soul a lift

Candy Paull

SPIRIT PRESS

101 Ways to Give Your Soul a Lift
ISBN: 1-40372-014-2

Published in 2006 by Spirit Press, an imprint of Dalmatian Press, LLC.
Copyright © 2006 Dalmatian Press, LLC. Franklin, Tennessee 37067.

Scripture quotations noted CEV are from *The Contemporary English Version*.
Copyright © 1991, 1992, 1995 by American Bible Society. Used by permission.

Scripture quotations marked THE MESSAGE are taken from *The Message*.
Copyright © by Eugene H. Peterson, 1993, 1994, 1995.
Used by permission of NavPress Publishing Group.

Scripture quotations marked NIV are taken from the *Holy Bible, New International
Version*®. NIV®. Copyright © 1973, 1978, 1984 by International Bible Society.
Used by permission of Zondervan Publishing House. All rights reserved.

Scripture quotations marked NKJV are taken from *The New King James Version*.
Copyright © 1979, 1980, 1982, Thomas Nelson, Inc.

Scripture quotations marked NLT are taken from the *Holy Bible, New Living
Translation*, Copyright © 1996. Used by permission of Tyndale House
Publishers, Inc., Wheaton, Illinois 60189. All rights reserved.

Scripture quotations noted NRSV are from the *New Revised Standard Version* of
the Bible, Copyright © 1989 by the Division of Christian Education of the
National Council of the Churches of Christ in the United States of America.
Used by permission. All rights reserved.

Editor: Lila Empson
Text Designer: Whisner Design Group

06 07 08 09 QSR 10 9 8 7 6 5 4 3 2 1

Printed in Canada

14932

*It is music's lofty
mission to shed
light on the depths
of the human heart.*
Robert Schumann

Contents

Contents continued...

Introduction

The soul encompasses the physical, spiritual, and emotional aspects of your inner self. In the rush and busyness of modern life, it's good to take time to nurture your soul. Nurturing the soul helps you see the spiritual in the midst of the ordinary and celebrate life as precious gift from God.

101 Ways to Give Your Soul a Lift offers simple ideas for taking soul breaks that relax and refresh the whole person. Take a drive down a winding country road, drink a soothing cup of tea, read a good book, spend time in prayer, get together with friends, and love life just a little more.

May you find delight for your soul in these pages, and may these meditations encourage you to cultivate a closer relationship with the God who loves to bless and heal your soul.

The LORD is my shepherd; I shall not want. He makes me to lie down in green pastures; He leads me beside the still waters. He restores my soul.

Psalm 23:1–3 NKJV

Life is the soul's nursery—its training place for the destinies of eternity.

William Makepeace Thackeray

Come to me, all you who are weary and burdened, and I will give you rest.

Matthew 11:28 NIV

Let Love Be Your Compass

A ship out on the ocean needs a compass to steer by. Even in the fog, one can locate true north and thus stay the ship on its course. Let love be the compass that points you in the right direction as you cross the sea of life. Let God's love rule in your heart, and make life choices that reflect love's highest priorities.

When you choose love, you make a choice that enriches your soul. At the end of your life, it won't be the big promotion or the career ladder climbed, but the love you shared that means the most.

love

Love from the center of who you are; don't fake it. Run for dear life from evil; hold on for dear life to good. Be good friends who love deeply.

Romans 12:9–10
THE MESSAGE

• Put love in action today with a simple act of kindness. When you express love to another person, you give your soul a lift as well as help others.

#2

Delight in the Small Things

> *The world will never starve for want of wonders.*
>
> G. K. Chesterton

delight

Life is made up of little things. Big events like births, graduations, weddings, and other milestones of life are important, but the greatest percentage of life is lived in the daily round. Take delight in the small gifts God sends you every day.

When you open your eyes in the morning, be fully aware of how good the bed feels. Enjoy the simple pleasures of the day—a friend's laughter, the sun breaking through the clouds, a favorite song on the radio, or a lover's kiss. Just before you go to sleep, think about the small delights of your day and thank God for them.

• Take a gratitude walk and thank God for the blessings you enjoy.

#3

Learn Something New

If you are feeling bored and tired, your horizons may be too small. Widen them by learning something new. Take a class in ceramics, world history, Thai cooking, dramatic arts, earth sciences, theology, music theory, archaeology, astrophysics, or any one of a thousand intriguing subjects. It's a big, beautiful, exciting world out there, so go explore.

Visiting a museum, taking a class, going to a workshop, or even reading books and magazines can not only expand your outer horizons, but it can also expand your inner horizons. You'll gain greater perspective on who you are and on the greatness of God's creation.

learn

If you have good sense, instruction will help you to have even better sense. And if you live right, education will help you to know even more.

Proverbs 9:9 CEV

• Sign up for a class or workshop. Read a book on a subject you know nothing about.

#4

Find a Prayer Partner

Again, I tell you that if two of you on earth agree about anything you ask for, it will be done for you by my Father in heaven.

Matthew 18:19 NIV

p a r t n e r

Prayer changes things. A prayer partner helps you grow in your prayer life by encouraging you to pray on a regular basis and sharing the excitement of answered prayer. Prayer partners become close friends, participating together in the joys and sorrows, ups and downs of life.

Finding a prayer partner and meeting together can be a life-changing experience. You'll be reminded that you are not alone. It is a comfort to know that someone else is praying for you, and it is good for the soul to pray for another person. When you hold each other up in prayer, your spiritual life is lifted to a new level.

• Ask a friend to be a prayer partner with you for a season. Meet regularly to report progress and pray together.

#5

Take Yourself on a Date

Setting aside regular dates with yourself is a wonderful way to nurture your soul. Even if you have a friend or loved one with whom you usually go out, going somewhere alone offers a different kind of soul experience. Think of this time on your own as a date with your creative spirit.

Take two hours out of your week to explore something that intrigues you. Visit a travel store, a botanical garden, a local landmark. Take in a movie. Bring a Bible along on a nature walk. Enjoy solitary pleasures that expand your mind, feed your spirit, and nurture your creative soul.

date

The opportunities for enjoyment in your life are limitless. If you feel you are not experiencing enough joy, you have only yourself to blame.

David E. Bresler

• Don't wait for someone else to call. Mark a date and time on your calendar and go do something you enjoy.

#6

Honor Tradition

> *Do not remove the ancient landmark that your ancestors set up.*
>
> Proverbs 22:28 NRSV

tradition

Traditions can be like markers in a field, offering perspective on the history of where you stand and where those who have gone before you marked boundaries. You can enrich your life and deepen your understanding by honoring tradition and the wisdom handed down from others.

Honoring tradition doesn't mean blindly following what has been handed down. It means integrating tradition into your life and even creating your own traditions. Family traditions, local traditions, and faith traditions all offer ways to bring more soul into everyday existence, connecting you with the dreams and ideals of those who lived before you.

• Check out the history and traditions of your faith. Learning the history behind favorite holidays and traditions will deepen your appreciation of them and make them more meaningful.

#7

Look for Angels

Angels are everywhere. You may have encountered one lately: the young man who stopped and changed a flat tire, the volunteer who carried bags of groceries into the local food bank, the kind stranger who gave accurate directions to the lost tourist. You may even have the opportunity sometime to be an "angel" for someone else, a messenger of God's love and care.

Look for angels around every corner. Seen and unseen, they are there to give your soul a lift and offer a helping hand. Even if you only hear the sound of wings brushing past, remember that God's angels are watching over you.

look

> *Angels mean messengers and ministers. Their function is to execute the plan of divine providence, even in earthly things.*
>
> Saint Thomas Aquinas

• Be alert for opportunities to be an "angel" in human form, for it will delight your soul to express God's love. Offer small services to others or use your helping hands at a local charity.

#8

Pitch In with Enthusiasm

Every impulse of generosity, when carried to fruition, gives a diastole to the soul which lifts it one step closer to the gates of heaven.

Kendall Weisiger

pitch in

God gave you hands that were meant to help others and to be used in creative ways. When you give enthusiastic help to others, it will lighten your heart and lighten their load. Your enthusiasm contributes as much as the actual work of your hands. God loves a cheerful giver—and so do other people.

Be generous with your time and talent. Don't be afraid to pitch in and help. You can help build a home, volunteer for a food drive, teach Sunday school, or pick up litter on a stretch of highway. Find a need you can meet and give the gift of yourself.

• Research volunteer opportunities. Pick something and give your time. Enjoy the pleasure of sharing your gifts and talents with others.

#9

Repair or Restore Something

Life is full of things that break. Yet you can repair or restore many things with just a little care and attention. You can reupholster an old chair, refinish a table, repair a favorite piece of clothing, and restore some discarded treasure to its rightful place of honor and use.

As you ply your needle, sand the surface of the wood, or paint a bright new color on a dingy, faded wall, you can meditate on how God repairs and restores your soul. God is the great restoration expert; he attends to broken hearts as carefully as you attend to broken objects.

repair

> *You refresh my life. You are true to your name, and you lead me along the right paths.*
>
> Psalm 23:3 CEV

• Pick one simple object to restore, repair, or renew. Enjoy the process of creating something useful or beautiful out of old discards.

#10

See the Splendor in the Ordinary

> *Beauty is the product of honest attention to the particular.*
>
> Richard Harries

ordinary

The Japanese have a term for something that is old and full of soul. *Wabi* refers to aged and imperfect items that have a weathered or worn patina. Ordinary things like an old teapot or a weathered wood fence have a value and nurture the soul in ways that slick new mass-produced things do not. Rustic handmade pottery, an old garden gate, or well-worn but still comfortable shoes all carry an ordinary splendor.

Ordinary splendor is found in people, as well as in things. Where some people may see wrinkles and old age, you can choose to see the beauty of an ordinary person reflecting the splendor of God.

• Find delight in the ordinary splendors in your life: a well-worn leather jacket, mismatched bone china cups and saucers, the old family Bible.

#11

Create Something That Is Satisfying

A beautiful hooked rug that took a year to make will be treasured for generations. A finely crafted grandfather clock that kept time in your father's house now marks the hours in your home. An heirloom quilt, a soft hand-knitted sweater, a family keepsake book, a ship's model, a lustrous old table—these are soul-satisfying creations that one generation to the next will treasure.

In this age of mass-produced plastics, it's refreshing to create something that will last for generations. Enjoy making something timeless that demands the best of your skill and craftsmanship. It will satisfy your soul to create something with lasting goodness.

create

> 'Tis God gives skill, but not without men's hands: He could not make Antonio Stradivari's violins without Antonio.
>
> George Eliot

• Create an object for the home that you would like future generations to cherish. It will satisfy your soul's need to create something lasting and beautiful.

#12

Listen to the Birds Sing

> *The flowers appear on the earth; the time of singing has come, and the voice of the turtledove is heard in our land.*
>
> Song of Solomon 2:12 NRSV

listen

Birdsong has inspired great composers. The birds sing the sun up on spring mornings and serenade creation through the hours of the day. Yet while these beautiful creatures sing praises to God, many people are shut up in houses and offices and factories and their own lives and are deaf to their music.

Go outside and listen to the birdsong chorus. Watch the winged life that goes on despite the stock market, the bad news, and the daily cares of life. Listening and watching will lift your spirit, remind you of eternal priorities, and put your human cares in a heavenly perspective.

• Put a birdfeeder in your backyard. As you watch the birds through the seasons, think about how God provides for you.

#13

Share Hugs Frequently

There are few things in life as comforting to the soul as giving and receiving a loving embrace. Hugs help you share burdens and demonstrate affection. A hearty hug welcomes; a tender embrace enfolds and comforts. Everyone needs the therapy of loving touch, and hugs are a perfect prescription for lifting the spirits.

Some people are more huggy-touchy than others, but even the shyest person enjoys genuine affection expressed in a warm and friendly hug. If you are feeling a bit blue and lonesome, seek out opportunities to hug and be hugged. Spread the love around. Value others as you value yourself, and enrich your soul.

hugs

He who loves his fellow man is loving God the best he can.

Alice Cary

• Give at least three people a caring embrace today. Let your hugs be expressions of God's love on earth.

#14

Cultivate a Sense of Awe and Wonder

> *I will praise You, for I am fearfully and wonderfully made; marvelous are Your works, and that my soul knows very well.*
>
> Psalm 139:14 NKJV

awe

It is easy to get caught up in the mundane aspects of life. You wake up, go to work, return home to routine chores, watch TV or read the paper, go to bed, and then do it all again the next day. But life is not just a round of chores and work. Life is a vast and amazing mystery.

The night sky is full of starry wonder. Take the time to look up. A kiss from your beloved, a rose blooming in the sun, a squirrel's antics—any of these can remind you of the mystery and greatness of God's creation.

• On a clear night, go outside and look up at the stars. Contemplate the vastness and mystery of space and creation.

#15

Move Your Body in Joyous Celebration

Toddlers know all about moving with joy. Everything is a new discovery to them. They are totally unselfconscious about moving their bodies and being just what God created them to be: some of the wiggliest creatures on the planet. You see the same youthfulness and love of life in puppies, kittens, and other baby animals.

Loosen up. God gave you a beautiful body. Take a few minutes to become like a child and move your body creatively. Put on some music, move your body, clap your hands, and celebrate the joy of living. Free your innermost self to delight in the exuberance of movement.

celebrate

> *You turned my wailing into dancing; you removed my sackcloth and clothed me with joy.*
>
> Psalm 30:11 NIV

• Enjoy being like a child again. Use your body to express your praise to God—dance, sing, lift your hands in praise, roll on the floor, run around in joy.

enrich

101 ways to give

delight

learn

pray

visit

your soul a lift

honor

look

help

#16

Let Music Soothe Your Soul

> *Music is the art of the prophets, the only art that can calm the agitations of the soul; it is one of the most magnificent and delightful presents God has given us.*
>
> Martin Luther

music

Music lifts you out of yourself. Whether it's an upbeat boogie-woogie or a shimmering symphonic tapestry of sound, this great gift of God is a perfect, portable soul break, going past the logic of the mind and nestling directly in the heart.

Listen to music in the car; sing as you do dishes; put on some gentle background music while you do your work. For an even more inspiring break away from the cares and problems of life, go to a live concert. Enjoy the experience of being in a room with others and sharing the soulful experience of listening to music together.

• Go to a concert and let the music take you away from your problems. Play soothing music at home for quiet contemplation.

#17

Praise God in Every Situation

It's easy to praise God when the sun shines and everything is going your way. Know, however, that God is with you in every situation, even in troubled times. When dark clouds cover the sun, look for the light and make a deliberate choice to praise God, no matter what your circumstances may be.

Every circumstance has its mercies and small blessings. When you lift praises to God, you inspire faith in your heart and teach your soul to trust. Develop your praise muscles in the good times so that you establish habits of praise and trust for the difficult times.

praise

We know that God is always at work for the good of everyone who loves him. They are the ones God has chosen for his purpose.

Romans 8:28 CEV

• Choose to praise God for everything that happens today, even for difficult or frustrating situations. Rest in God's ability to work all things together for good.

#18

Work with Your Hands

> *Real joy comes not from ease or riches or from the praise of men, but from doing something worthwhile.*
>
> Wilfred T. Grenfell

work

Take a moment to look at your hands. These are God's beautiful works of art, created so that humanity can create. Think about how your hands help you do so many wonderful things: stroke a cat's soft fur, dig in the garden, chop vegetables, caress a loved one, build a strong fence, repair a car, write a letter, throw a pot, knit a sweater, or reach out in love.

Working with your hands on creative projects offers the satisfaction of a job well done and expresses God-given creativity. Using the gift of hands, you create gifts for those you love.

• Set aside some time this weekend to use your hands to dig in the garden, build something useful, or work on a handcrafted project. Work well done inspires the soul.

#19

Take a Soul Vacation

There are vacations—and then there are soul vacations. A soul vacation can happen in a few minutes, a few hours, or a few days. Instead of packing your bags and heading for distant destinations, you can indulge your imagination, spend some time in contemplation, and satisfy your soul with the honey sweetness of the present moment.

A soul vacation makes much of small things. Enjoy a good book that takes you on inner adventures. Contemplate the wonders of God's creation by watching a bee browse in the heart of a flower. Take a walk in the woods. Sit and think about life.

vacation

> *The windows of my soul I throw Wide open to the sun.*
> John Greenleaf Whittier

• Set aside a soul vacation for an afternoon. Do something you enjoy that also gives you time to contemplate what God is doing in your life.

#20

Make Room for the New

> *To be made new in the attitude of your minds; and to put on the new self, created to be like God in true righteousness and holiness.*
>
> Ephesians 4:23–24
> NIV

new

If too much dust has settled on your things, there's probably dust settling on your life as well. When you move, clean, and clear out to make room for something new, it gives your soul more room to breathe.

This holds true not only for your external home, but also for the inner heart. You can do the same with your thoughts as you sort and rearrange furnishings. Do a little housekeeping of the soul. Sweep out old prejudices and throw open the windows of your mind. Give your soul a lift by receiving the fresh breezes of the new things God wants to bring into your life.

• Pass on to others books that you have enjoyed. Make room for new books to nurture your soul with new ideas.

#21

Plant a Tree

Planting a tree is an act of faith that expresses a deep hope for the future. It can be a gift to your children and your children's children. Johnny Appleseed planted apple trees across the frontier so that future generations would enjoy them. Timber companies plant trees so that they can be harvested thirty, forty, or a hundred years from now.

Even if you can't plant a tree, you can plant a seed of faith in your heart. A vision of faith that works today for a good that extends far into the future declares the soul's trust in the providence of God.

plant

> *Even if I knew that tomorrow the world would go to pieces, I would still plant my apple tree.*
>
> Martin Luther

• Plant a seed and make it the tangible symbol of a seed of faith you're planting in your heart.

#22
Go Fishing

> *To go fishing is the chance to wash one's soul with pure air, with the rush of the brook, or with the shimmer of the sun on blue water.*
>
> Herbert Hoover

fish

Jesus was a fisherman. He was intimately familiar with the hard work of a fisherman's life. But he would also have experienced quiet moments of contemplation watching the sun sparkle on the Sea of Galilee, waiting for fish, being with the disciples, and listening to his Father's voice. Fishermen know that going fishing is about more than just catching fish.

Go fishing—either literally or figuratively. Quiet hours spent in nature slow you down, giving your soul time to listen to God and to think about your life. You may not catch any fish, but you will probably catch a fresh perspective on life.

• Spend some quiet time fishing or simply contemplating the beauties of creation and listening to God.

#23

Remember the Good Times

The soul loves to remember the past and color dreams of the future with it. When you concentrate on happy memories, you renew hope, for these memories remind you of how rich you are in friends, family, and loving relationships. Let memories of good times inspire you to create more good times with loved ones.

Open the pages of a scrapbook or look at old photos. Remember good times gone by, dearly beloved friends and family, and the wonderful moments when you were all together. Feast your soul on happy memories and thank God for the blessings you have experienced in this life.

remember

> *Remember His marvelous works which He has done, His wonders, and the judgments of His mouth.*
>
> Psalm 105:5 NKJV

• Get together with family or friends for a reunion. Enjoy reliving old memories and sharing favorite stories.

#24

Celebrate Your Senses

> *A sound mind in a sound body is a short but full description of a happy state in this world.*
>
> John Locke

celebrate

The five senses are a mysterious and wonderful gift from God. Though we use our senses for survival, the rich tapestry of sensation is full of pleasure, too. The scent of piney woods, the flaming colors of sunrise, the touch of a beloved's hand, the sound of beautiful music, and the taste of sweet ripe melon—it is as if God continually woos your soul as he pours his love out to you through the world he created.

Celebrate your senses and let God whisper his love to you in the simple daily pleasures of scent, sight, touch, sound, and taste.

• Take special notice of all the beautiful sensations and delights of sight, sound, taste, touch, and scent that the day brings.

#25

Learn About Different Cultures

You live in a world that is becoming more connected all the time. Today you have unparalleled opportunities to experience different cultures and get to know people of all kinds. It is exciting to find out how they grew up, what kind of foods they eat, what they learned in school, and how they view your culture.

Variety is spice for the life of the soul. Get out of your rut and expand your horizons by investigating another culture. From a meal at a local ethnic restaurant to a trip abroad, learning about different cultures gives you greater understanding of your own culture. Variety is spice for the soul.

learn

> *May God be gracious to us and bless us and make his face to shine upon us, (Selah) that your way may be known upon earth, your saving power among all nations.*
>
> Psalm 67:1–2 NRSV

• Try a new dish at an ethnic restaurant and enjoy a taste from another culture.

#26

Trust in God as Your Provider

> *Providence is the care God takes of all existing things.*
> Saint John of Damascus

trust

Providence is the divine care of God and his perfect timing in your life. When you are wondering how you will meet bills and obligations, or what will happen in a troublesome situation, take a step back and focus on the God who provides for you, instead of on the need that concerns you.

God's provision is never too early and never too late, but always on time. You may not receive it when you desire it, but you will receive it when you need it. Trust God and face troubles peacefully, knowing that divine love will provide what you need at the perfect time.

• Be an agent of God's providence and answer someone else's prayer with a generous gift of help.

#27

Read History

Reading history as an adult takes you far beyond the dry history lessons of school. It's an exciting and enriching story that introduces you to complex men and women who lived through turbulent times. The times may have been different, but people wrestle with the same problems today. You can find inspiration and warning from the people and events of the past, and you can gain a wiser perspective on your own life and times.

Read history and discover your spiritual roots, as well. Church history and biblical archaeology help you learn from people who lived in other times, offering inspiration and perspective for your own life.

read

> *Our LORD, I will remember the things you have done, your miracles of long ago.*
>
> Psalm 77:11 CEV

• Read a book about an era in history that interests you or visit a local historical site and be inspired by how others met the challenges of life.

#28

Be a Child for a Day

He called a little child and had him stand among them. And he said: "I tell you the truth, unless you change and become like little children, you will never enter the kingdom of heaven."

Matthew 18:2–3 NIV

child

Childhood goes to the roots of your soul. Reclaim your childlike wisdom, and pretend to be a child for a day. Reconnecting with the joys and feelings of childhood connects you with the deepest roots of your soul.

If you don't remember how to be a child, invite a youngster to spend the day with you. Indulge in favorite childhood activities. Go to the zoo, roll in the grass, play with other children. Have a day of pure fun. Let childhood memories and experiences give you a new perspective on what it means to be grown up. Think of ways your adult life can reflect the kingdom of heaven.

• Watch children at play. Think about ways you can cultivate a childlike spirit, imagination, and openness.

#29

Be a Beginner Again

Cultivate childlike wisdom by being a beginner again. Every great artist knows that creating something fresh requires an open mind and a willingness to try something new. Creating a soulful life includes being open to new ideas, new experiences, and fresh perspectives.

In the beginner's mind, there are endless possibilities. In the mind of the expert, there are a limited number of answers. Instead of basing your decisions on what you know of the past, explore unknown possibilities. Break out of the box of old limitations and approach life with the attitude that you are a beginner and can learn something new.

beginner

Anyone who stops learning is old, whether twenty or eighty. Anyone who keeps learning today is young. The greatest thing in life is to keep your mind young.

Henry Ford

• Get together with a friend and brainstorm possibilities for each other. Let your imagination run free, and remember that there are no wrong answers.

#30

Seek the Pearl of Great Price

The kingdom of heaven is like a merchant seeking beautiful pearls, who, when he had found one pearl of great price, went and sold all that he had and bought it.

Matthew 13:45–46
NKJV

seek

The love of God is an extravagant love. Your soul longs for such an extravagant love—a love that is willing to let go of everything in order to possess that which is beyond price.

If you have been settling for less than this great, extravagant love, consider the worth of the things you hold to so tightly, and compare them to the priceless gift of God's love. Choosing to cultivate love will inspire you and lift your soul. Spend more time cultivating your spiritual life and seek God's love. Decide what you're willing to give to seek and possess the pearl of great price.

• Look at where you put your time and energy. Think of one change you could make to pursue the higher priorities of love. Do it.

#31

Spend Quiet Time with God

It is good for the soul to withdraw from the busyness of life to spend quiet time alone with God. Prayer, meditation, and silence lift the heart and mind with visions of higher things. If you cultivate a regular time to meet with God, it will soon become the lifeline that offers a larger perspective of who you are and what you are meant to accomplish in life.

You can start by learning to become quiet before God, stilling your distracting thoughts, and focusing on his greatness. Meditating on a Scripture verse can focus your thoughts. Over time you'll develop an intimate communion with God.

quiet

> *It is in silence that God is known, and through mysteries that He declares Himself.*
> Robert Hugh Benson

• Set aside regular times for prayer and silence. Try to meet God at the same time and place every day, even if it's only for a few quiet minutes.

listen

101 ways to give

praise

reach

read

breathe

your soul a lift

plant

remember

celebrate

#32

Appreciate Art

> *In all ranks of life the human heart yearns for the beautiful, and the beautiful things that God makes are his gifts to all alike.*
>
> Harriet Beecher Stowe

art

The soul longs for beauty and to express itself through beauty. When Solomon built the temple for God, he brought the best craftsmen and artists to create the beautiful building. Art, architecture, music, and human creativity express the soul of the artist and reflect the created world that is an expression of the Great Artist.

Cultivate an appreciation of art. It will enrich your life, expand your understanding, and feed your soul. Enjoy a trip to an art museum, hang meaningful pictures on your walls, or take a class in art appreciation. Make art an essential part of your life. It will nurture your soul.

• Create art as a form of meditation: make a collage, paint or draw, and express yourself through creativity.

#33

Be a Tourist in Your Hometown

Do you appreciate the place where you live? Do you know its history? Where would you go if you wanted to show an out-of-town friend the local sights? If you travel hundreds of miles to see the sights of some other part of the country but neglect the treasures waiting for you in your own backyard, you are missing out on wonderful adventures.

Play tourist without leaving home. Check out a museum that tells the history of your area. Look for local color in a finger-lickin' good chicken or crab shack. Appreciate the place where you live and expand your soul's perspective with a little fun.

tourist

The world is so full of a number of things, I'm sure we should all be as happy as kings.

Robert Louis Stevenson

• Take time for fun. Play tourist in your own city and explore the sights. Lift your soul by visiting a local museum, a favorite restaurant, a park, or a historical site.

#34

Collect the Beautiful and Unique

> *I have filled him with the Spirit of God, giving him great wisdom, intelligence, and skill in all kinds of crafts. . . . He is skilled in cutting and setting gemstones and in carving wood. Yes, he is a master at every craft!*
>
> Exodus 31:3, 5 NLT

collect

When directions were given for the high priests' garments and the design of the temple in Jerusalem, beauty and rarity and the skill of the craftsmen were all essential parts of God's directions. A soulful life includes valuing expressions of skill and beauty; making, using, and enjoying the creations of gifted craftspeople and artists.

Look for beautiful and unique things. Collect them for your home, give them as gifts. Take pleasure in the design and color of an exquisite piece of jewelry, a finely crafted piece of furniture, a carefully stitched handmade quilt, an earthy woven basket, or a lovingly hand-carved walking stick.

• Go to a crafts fair and enjoy seeing all the creative and artistic items that people make and sell.

#35

Create a Scrapbook

Life is full of memories and milestones. Births, weddings, and anniversaries mark the milestones of life, as do the daily pleasures and treasures that come with a full and busy life. Savor the moment by setting aside mementos and putting them in a scrapbook. Then you'll have a soul-satisfying memory book to help you measure your growth and remind you of bygone eras in your life.

As you sort through old photographs, remember the good times and the people who are dear to your heart. A scrapbook is a great way to rekindle happy memories and inspire your soul.

savor

God gave us memories so we could have roses in winter.

Author Unknown

• Create a memory book that keeps track of the events of your life through photos, letters, memorabilia, and diaries.

#36

Live Each Moment as a Blessing

The LORD will command His lovingkindness in the daytime, and in the night His song shall be with me—a prayer to the God of my life.

Psalm 42:8 NKJV

live

Every moment is precious. Each day is a gift from God. Instead of anticipating the future or regretting the past, focus on what is happening in your life at this moment in time. You'll discover that this moment contains many blessings that usually go unnoticed.

God is in the details—and the details of even the simplest daily act are rich with beauty and blessing. Accept everything that comes your way as a blessing. Count difficulties as blessings in disguise, trusting that you will one day understand. God blesses each moment of your life. Thank him for each blessed one.

• Pay attention to what is happening in this minute. Be aware of all the good that surrounds you right now and thank God for it.

#37

Develop a Passion for Excellence

The violinist moves the audience with the transcendent perfection of his art. The Olympic skater glides across the ice with grace and ease. Tiny, even stitches in an heirloom quilt show the care and skill employed in its making. Excellence inspires and lifts the soul to higher levels of enjoyment.

Develop a passion for excellence in your own life. The Olympic athlete or star musician spent hours in practice and preparation to become that good. Invest some time in becoming excellent at a craft or skill you love. When you do something well, you enjoy doing it more and find it more rewarding.

excellence

The quality of a person's life is in direct proportion to their commitment to excellence, regardless of their chosen field of endeavor.

Vince Lombardi

• Satisfy your soul by taking the time to practice and hone a skill that you would like to develop or improve.

#38

Go Exploring

> *The steps of the godly are directed by the LORD. He delights in every detail of their lives.*
>
> Psalm 37:23 NLT

explore

Children start out in life eager to explore. They are not afraid of mistakes and are always ready to embrace a new idea or try something new. You can take some of that childlike openness and apply it to your life. If you are willing to go exploring, you can have all kinds of adventures.

A trip may include flat tires as well as rest stops and viewpoints. But that's all part of the adventure. If you knew what was going to happen, it wouldn't be an adventure. With God as your guide you'll enjoy the ride and find your way safely home.

• Take a drive down a winding country road and let it lead you to new adventures.

#39

Pause and Reflect

If your day is hectic and scattered, pull yourself together by taking a few moments for reflection. Though there was much work to do, Jesus would steal away from the crowds to pray and refresh his spirit. He knew that time out for reflection was important for accomplishing the work of the kingdom.

Take a few minutes to pause and reflect in your day. Give yourself time to think and your soul some space to breathe. A little bit of time for reflection will renew your perspective, refresh you, and give you more energy to accomplish your goals and meet the needs of others.

p a u s e

All men's miseries derive from not being able to sit quiet in a room alone.

Blaise Pascal

• Take at least one fifteen-minute break in the midst of a busy day to pause, reflect, and give yourself time to think.

#40

Call a Friend Today

The impulse of love that leads us to the doorway of a friend is the voice of God within, and we need not be afraid to follow it.

Agnes Sanford

call

Friends make life worth living. Spending time with a friend can give your soul a lift. Shared laughter, talking about what's happening in your life, and just getting another perspective on what's going on in the world can lighten any day.

Don't let a busy life prevent you from spending time with friends. You need your friends and your friends need you. Stay in touch with friends. Let them know you think of them often. Make an appointment to get together and talk about what's going on in each other's lives. Let your friends know that you value them and want to be with them.

• Make a call or go by to see a friend and catch up on each other's life.

#41

Seek Serendipity

Serendipity is the faculty of finding valuable or agreeable things not sought for. Cultivate an attitude of faith and optimism. If you look for serendipity, you'll probably find it. Be flexible and spontaneous. Enjoy the unexpected—it may be God's way of getting your attention.

Be open to the deeper intuitions of the soul. If something intrigues you or draws your attention, explore that interest. It may lead you to a completely new adventure. Trust God to find inventive ways to bring love, joy, and life lessons to you. Appreciate delightful surprises, knowing you are guided every step of the way.

seek

I will lead the blind by ways they have not known, along unfamiliar paths I will guide them; I will turn the darkness into light before them and make the rough places smooth.

Isaiah 42:16 NIV

• Explore an intriguing specialty shop, such as a fabric store, hardware store, spa or salon, travel store, candle shop, or import store.

#42

Loosen Up and Laugh

> *A good laugh is sunshine in the house.*
> William Makepeace Thackeray

laugh

Laughter is good medicine and a great healer. Laughter renews your perspective and makes you feel better. Laughter helps you find your playful, uncomplicated side and lose the rigid, uncompromising adult part of you that can become too serious for its own good. It's a release for the soul, the part of you that delights in the absurd.

Get together with friends and toss around a few comic ideas: tell bad jokes, make up silly stories, play childhood games. Read a funny book or watch a stand-up comedian. Pop some corn, rent a movie or two, and spend an evening laughing at your favorite comedies.

• Go to a toy store and find some inexpensive, fun things that will spark laughter when you get together with friends.

#43

Memorize Inspiring Words

You can find instant inspiration in quotes and Bible verses. When you feed your mind with inspirational words, you're preparing for the future. Memorizing promises from the Bible or wise quotes from people you admire is like storing up honey. Those sweet, wise words will be there when you're facing tough times and difficult decisions.

Memorize a Bible verse or even an entire section of Scripture. Look for inspirational books that can lift you up when you're discouraged and give you new insights on how to live your life. Committing inspirational words to memory is a powerful tool for self-transformation.

memorize

I have gained perfect freedom by following your teachings.

Psalm 119:45 CEV

• Pick a Bible promise (example: Psalm 91:1–2) and post it near your bathroom mirror. Memorize it for future reference.

#44

Pamper Yourself

> *Thus said the Lord GOD, the Holy One of Israel: In returning and rest you shall be saved; in quietness and in trust shall be your strength.*
>
> Isaiah 30:15 NRSV

pamper

It's important to take care of yourself. Yet if you're like most people, you probably put yourself last on the to-do list. Taking time out to relax, refresh, and de-stress is an important part of nurturing your soul. If you're exhausted and frazzled, you won't do anybody any good, including yourself.

Take time for a warm, soothing herbal bath. Get a massage. Take a nap. Take a full day off—sleep in, read, putter, relax. Put work aside, save the chores till later, and go out for a walk. Pamper yourself, and it will pay dividends of energy and renewed perspective.

• Set aside a full day off as a Sabbath for your soul. Rest, meditate, relax, get away—do whatever you want to do.

#45

Curl Up with a Good Book

Curling up with a good book is a childhood pleasure that you can revisit. Reading stretches your soul by offering new ideas and experiences. Having acres of time to immerse yourself in a rousing adventure story or hours to indulge in a passion for understanding a favorite subject creates a mini-vacation in a busy life.

Take a good book with you on vacation—every summer booksellers release a new crop of good "beach reads." And you don't have to wait for vacation. Even if you only have a half-hour, you can still savor a taste of the luxury of getting lost in a good book.

book

Everywhere I have sought rest and not found it, except sitting in a corner by myself with a little book.

Thomas à Kempis

• Go to the library or bookstore and find a book that inspires you or offers a refreshing perspective on life.

#46

Breathe In, Breathe Out

We plan the way we want to live, but only GOD makes us able to live it.

Proverbs 16:9
THE MESSAGE

breathe

Do you often find yourself taking quick, shallow breaths? This kind of breathing stems from and creates tension. Relax your body and calm your nerves by taking deep breaths that reach deep down into the belly.

Breathing deeply draws oxygen into your body. Take a deep breath, and then exhale fully with a gentle sigh. This helps the body relax, which will lead the mind into a more flexible and open state.

As you take deep, relaxing breaths, use this as a meditation for your spirit. Breathe in the love of God. Breathe out all your fears, doubts, and regrets.

• Take a deep breath and draw in the energy and renewal you need. Exhale, and release that which no longer serves you.

#47

Be Aware

Life is rich and beautiful, full of wonders. But you have to develop the eyes to see the wonders; you have to attune your soul to the works of God that surround you. Becoming aware is a process of waking up and learning to notice the treasures that you usually miss.

Be aware of tiny details. What do you see when you wake up? What do you hear, smell, sense? Pay attention to what is happening around you. Look at a loved one's face as if you are seeing him or her for the first time. Extend your awareness to God. What is he whispering to you today?

> *For lack of attention, a thousand forms of loveliness elude us every day.*
>
> Evelyn Underhill

• Keep a notepad handy and list "Things I've noticed this day that I've missed until today."

express

101 ways to give

create

appreciate

collect

savor

your soul a lift

discover

develop

explore

#48

Awaken the Dawn

> *Awake, my soul!*
> *Awake, harp and*
> *lyre! I will awaken*
> *the dawn.*
>
> Psalm 57:8 NIV

awaken

There is something about the early morning, before the sun has come over the horizon and before the sleeping world awakens. It is a perfect time to be alone with God, to watch the sun rise and the day begin. Though getting up early can be a stretch, it will reward your soul with a memorable time of devotion and praise.

In winter darkness, light a candle as you wait for the light to dawn in the gray morning. In summer, go outside to hear the birds sing and the natural world come to life. You'll always treasure the mornings you awakened with the dawn.

• Set your alarm clock for earlier than usual tomorrow morning so you can watch the sun rise. Pray and meditate on this dawn as a symbol of new beginnings in your personal life.

#49

Watch the Sun Go Down

Summer sunsets can be glorious, with soft breezes and firefly twilights mirroring the stars on earth. Fall colors blaze even brighter in the setting sun, while winter sunsets, though brief, can bring a spot of color to a gray day. People gather at favorite views to enjoy the sunset and unwind at the end of the day.

Take time to watch the sun go down. It's a natural break in the rhythm of the day. Watching sunsets is good for the soul. It gives you a breathing space to contemplate the day, prepare for evening's rest, and thank God for his care.

watch

The day is done, and the darkness Falls from the wings of Night, As a feather is wafted downward From an eagle in his flight.

Henry Wadsworth Longfellow

- Sit on your porch or deck and watch the sun go down and the twilight come. Or take a picnic supper to enjoy at a favorite sunset vista.

#50

Exercise Your Imagination

> *The mind is good—God put it there. He gave us our heads, and it was not his intention that our heads would function just as a place to hang a hat.*
>
> A. W. Tozer

imagine

The imaginative mind is a gift from God. Don't be afraid to use it. From pencils and paper clips to rockets and skyscrapers, every invention began in someone's mind. Use your imagination as inspiration. Dare to dream, for dreams nurture the soul and inspire you to move beyond the current limitations of your life.

You can invent a better life for yourself and others by exercising your imagination. You can create a beautiful piece of art, a more effective way of accomplishing a task, or a better way to serve your community.

• Instead of imagining worst-case scenarios, use your imagination to seek innovative solutions to a problem that has been bothering you.

#51

Go Barefoot in the Grass

When Moses encountered the burning bush, the Lord told him to take off his shoes, for Moses was standing on holy ground. You may not be confronted by a burning bush or hear a voice from heaven telling you to remove your sandals, but you can choose to look at the world soulfully, to see common earth as holy ground, and to remind yourself of the Creator God who made it and all its creatures.

Children find wonder in simple things like soft green grass and squishy mud. Go barefoot and feel the earth; wonder with a childlike heart at creation's intimate foot-level beauties and oddities.

barefoot

> God replied, "Don't come any closer. Take off your sandals—the ground where you are standing is holy."
>
> Exodus 3:5 CEV

• Take your shoes off and go barefoot in the grass. Paddle your feet in a mud puddle. Or feel the sand between your toes.

#52
Get in the Flow

> *He guides the humble in what is right and teaches them his way.*
>
> Psalm 25:9 NIV

flow

Watch a stream tumbling over and past the rocks. The rocks are in the path, but the water doesn't resist, it just flows around the rocks. The water has its own momentum, moving irresistibly downstream to its eventual ocean destination.

Life can be like a stream. Sometimes there are obstacles, but instead of resisting, go with the flow. Give your soul a rest from trying too hard. Trust God to take you where you need to go, using all circumstances to guide you. Trust his love to carry you through the rapids and take you to your destination.

• The next time you find yourself resisting current circumstances, ask yourself how God might be leading you within and through them.

#53

Cultivate Roses

The rose is the queen of flowers. Whether you are fortunate enough to cultivate a garden full of them or able only to buy a single stem from your local florist, the rose blossom speaks to your heart, whispering secrets of the soul and stories of creation.

Look at a single rosebud. See how the petals unfurl in ever-widening circles. Hold the rose up to the sunlight and notice the way each petal glistens with life and color. Meditate on the image of the rose and take pleasure in the beauty God created. Think about how you are gradually unfolding, like the rose, in God's garden.

cultivate

A rose is more than just a flower. It brings with it a glimmer of the whys and wherefores of Creation.

Cyril Fletcher

• Cultivate a rosebush. You can grow a full-size one in your garden or buy a miniature rosebush for a sunny window sill.

#54
Enjoy the View

By taking a long and thoughtful look at what God has created, people have always been able to see what their eyes as such can't see: eternal power, for instance, and the mystery of his divine being.

Romans 1:20
THE MESSAGE

view

Every moment of your life offers an opportunity to see the unfolding wonders of creation and the ways of God. Everything you look at can be a glimpse into God's glory. A mountaintop experience in a beautiful natural setting inspires the soul to worship; the view from your daily life offers humbler opportunities to appreciate the works and ways of God.

Human faces reflect God's glory and creativity. Enjoy the view from a busy sidewalk as all the people pass by. God loves them all. Then take another look at your own face in the mirror, and remember that God loves you, too.

• Go to a busy airport, train station, mall, or city sidewalk and watch the passing parade of people. Meditate on God's love for each individual.

#55

To Thine Own Dreams Be True

God planted dreams in your heart. You dared to dream them when you were a child. If you set those dreams aside when you reached adulthood, it's time to revisit them again. Childhood dreams can be keys to new adventures that would satisfy your soul.

You may have dreamed of being an artist, an astronaut, a farmer, an architect, or a doctor. Though you may not go to medical school or into outer space, you can take the essence of the original dream and make it yours. Take up painting, study the stars, design and plant a garden, or volunteer at your local hospital.

be true

How much better to know that we have dared to live our dreams than to live our lives in a lethargy of regret.

Gilbert E. Kaplan

• List five enjoyable things you've always wanted to do but, for one reason or another, have not yet done. Go do one of them.

#56
Be Brave

> *I command you — be strong and courageous! Do not be afraid or discouraged. For the LORD your God is with you wherever you go.*
>
> Joshua 1:9 NLT

brave

Courage comes when you step out and do something you are afraid to do. When you are brave enough to face your fears and do the thing that seems most impossible, you have made a choice that will strengthen your faith and open new possibilities in your life.

Instead of allowing your fears to stop you from doing what you love to do or what you know you should do, be brave and take a step of faith. Trusting God's guidance, choose to move beyond your fears. An act of courage can create confidence, build your faith, and inspire others.

• The next time you are feeling shy in a crowd, take a small step of faith and introduce yourself to someone you don't know.

#57

Take Time for Tea

The British know the secret of lifting your spirits. Teatime is a refreshing afternoon ceremony that relaxes and renews, giving you a welcome break that offers energy to take you through the rest of your day. A leisurely "cuppa" can soothe or invigorate, depending on the kind of tea you choose.

Make teatime a nurturing ritual in your day. Enjoy a cup of English Breakfast tea with cream to wake you in the morning. Make a pot of Earl Grey for an afternoon pick-me-up. Cool down with a southern favorite, iced tea. Savor a soothing herbal tisane before going to bed.

tea

With tea amuses the evening, with tea solaces the midnight, with tea welcomes the morning.

Samuel Johnson

• Invite a friend to share teatime with you and catch up on the latest news over a cup of steaming tea or a cooling glass of iced tea.

#58

Light Your Inner Fire

We pray that you'll have the strength to stick it out over the long haul — not the grim strength of gritting your teeth but the glory-strength God gives.

Colossians 1:11
THE MESSAGE

light

The inner fire will light your way even in the darkest times. This inner fire is a passion for God and is your connection to him. God created you to live life fully, in a joyful and adventurous partnership with him. Nurture the inner spark, and it will be the fire that keeps your heart warm and glowing with love.

Spend quiet time alone with God, warming your heart in his presence. Learn to love God more deeply and let the love you find with him be the fire that fuels your day.

• Create a personal space for worship and meditation. Include things that remind you that God is with you wherever you go.

#59

Collect Seashells and Pine Cones

The elegant curl and curve of a conch held up to the ear brings the sound of the sea to you, no matter how far inland you live. The symmetrical beauty of a pine cone is a beautiful brown spiral of seed potential. A colorful stone, eons in the making, now speaks to you of God's ongoing creation.

Collect and enjoy things from nature. Natural things can teach you about God and about your potential for growth and change. Stones, leaves, flowers, shells, and other bits of nature offer simple reminders to meditate on God's creative work within your soul.

collect

One cannot collect all the beautiful shells on the beach. One can collect only a few, and they are more beautiful if they are few.

Anne Morrow
Lindbergh

• Go for a walk in nature—seashore, woods, riverbank, meadow—and find a beautiful stone, shell, leaf, or flower. Rejoice in God's creation.

#60

Applaud God

Praise not merely expresses, but completes the enjoyment; it is its appointed consummation. . . . In commending us to glorify him, God is inviting us to enjoy him.
C. S. Lewis

applaud

The Psalms are full of praises to God. "Let every living, breathing creature praise GOD!" (Psalm 150:6 THE MESSAGE). Praise is a natural response to the greatness and goodness of God. Whether you see his hand in the outward creation or experience the touch of his love in your soul, when you encounter that greatness, something inside breaks into praise and applause.

Lift your spirits by giving God glory and praise. Applaud God and his works. When you see a beautiful sunset, clap your hands with appreciation. When you hold a newborn baby, croon your praises to the Creator. Enjoy God and applaud.

• Write a poem, sing a song of praise, create a gratitude journal, or worship with others to express your appreciation and thankfulness to God.

#61

Know When Enough Is Enough

Advertisers urge you to buy more, do more, have more. Wisdom, however, teaches that less can be more. Knowing when enough is enough helps you make wiser and more powerful choices.

Whether you've packed your closet with too many things or crammed your schedule with too many appointments, the less-is-more approach to life can help you revise your priorities and make space in your world for the things that count. Simplify your life by saying no to more. Create open spaces in your home that rest your eyes with elegant emptiness. Make room for God to fill your soul with his enough.

enough

> *Why is everyone hungry for more? "More, more," they say. "More, more." I have God's more-than-enough.*
>
> Psalm 4:6
> THE MESSAGE

• Schedule appointments in your calendar for "doing nothing," and give your soul time to breathe and space to stretch.

#62
Take a Nap

> *I can lie down and sleep soundly because you, LORD, will keep me safe.*
>
> Psalm 4:8 CEV

nap

You don't have to be a child to enjoy the benefits of a good nap. Adults, too, can benefit from naps. Allow the simple gift of sleep to heal your body and knit your soul back together. Latin Americans practice the wisdom of the siesta, and you can adapt this beneficial habit to your own life.

Taking a nap relaxes you. A few minutes of catnapping or an hour of sleeping in the afternoon is like an extra helping of healing and refreshment. Nurture body and soul with gentle nap therapy, and see if you don't enjoy life a little more.

• The next time you are dragging in the afternoon, take a quick cat nap. Or give yourself the luxury of a long, leisurely nap on your day off.

#63

Make Peace with Imperfection

The snowy perfection of a white blouse is marred by a small stain. The untouched perfection of a snow-covered lawn is suddenly covered with the tracks of children's boots. The perfect new romance runs into the first argument.

Relax. That's life. Trying to keep everything perfect is an exercise in futility. Trying to *be* perfect is impossible. Instead, look at imperfections as part of the process of living. You can wash out stains. The pristine snowfall will become slush. Relationships go through seasons of growth and change. Enjoy the soulful imperfection of being present in the mess and majesty of life.

peace

> *Demand perfection in yourself and you'll seldom attain it. Fear of making a mistake is the biggest single cause of making one. Relax—pursue excellence, not perfection.*
>
> Bud Winter

• Enjoy the comfort and freedom of old clothes (like your favorite pair of jeans) that are no longer "perfect" but perfectly usable.

awaken

101 ways to give

imagine

invent

wonder

watch

your soul a lift

meditate

think

dare

#64

Learn to Play an Instrument

> It is music's lofty mission to shed light on the depths of the human heart.
>
> Robert Schumann

play

You're never too old to learn to play a musical instrument. Though many people and almost all performers start young, the pleasures of learning an instrument offer lessons for the soul at any age. From the very first time you touch the instrument to the day you are able to play it competently, it will enrich your enjoyment of all music and teach you about beauty and creativity.

The discipline of practice teaches you about the rewards of patient effort. Learning how to bring music out in your instrument offers insight into how you can make heavenly music out of the daily stuff of life.

• Go to a music or piano store and try out a few instruments. Rent an instrument and take a few lessons before you commit to buying.

#65

Escape to the Wild Places

Past the fast-food restaurants, strip malls, and billboards, there is a world of untouched beauty that speaks to the soul. The primal creation, the wild places—mountain, forest, untamed shore, winding riverfront, vast desert—speak of God's glory and remind you that this is a very large and beautiful world.

Escape to the wild places to renew your spirit. Let the wind blow through your hair and whisper secrets of creation to your heart. Enjoy being away from all man-made structures and in the midst of God-created beauty. You'll return to your daily life with a wider perspective.

escape

Touch the earth, love the earth, honour the earth, her plains, her valleys, her hills, and her seas; rest your spirit in her solitary places.

Henry Beston

• Take a Bible or spiritual reading with you on a wilderness hike. The words will have a different resonance for you when read in nature.

#66

Give Anonymously

> *When you give to the needy, do not let your left hand know what your right hand is doing, so that your giving may be in secret. Then your Father, who sees what is done in secret, will reward you.*
>
> Matthew 6:3–4 NIV

give

It's fun to give and have your gift acknowledged. It's even more fun to be an anonymous donor. There is something soul satisfying about a gift with no strings attached, no thank-you expected, and no need to be recognized. In some ways, giving anonymously mirrors the generous and unseen hand of God.

Think of creative ways to give anonymously. Leave a basket of goodies on the doorstep of a needy family. Tuck cash or a money order or a gift certificate in an envelope and send it. Look for ways to give, and you will receive a hundredfold back from God.

• Give anonymously by tucking a twenty-dollar bill in an envelope and sending it with an unsigned note of encouragement. (Remember: no return address!)

#67

Buy Yourself a Bouquet

There are days for single roses or for wildflowers picked from the side of the road. But some days require a little more abundance. A big bouquet is a great once-in-a-while splurge that is a lovely reminder of the abundance and generosity of God.

A big bouquet gives you the pleasure of arranging flowers for yourself—and for others. With a plenitude of flowers, sharing generously just comes naturally. You can enjoy the whole bouquet in one arrangement, or you can divide it; some to keep and some to give. A big bouquet offers a feast of loveliness for the soul.

bouquet

Flowers are the sweetest things that God ever made, and forgot to put a soul into.
Henry Ward Beecher

• The next time you pass a flower shop, stop in and buy a big bouquet. Share some of it with others.

#68

Choose Happiness

I'm happy from the inside out, and from the outside in, I'm firmly formed.

Psalm 16:9
THE MESSAGE

choose

Happiness can be a choice. While some choose to look at the dark side of life, a person who chooses happiness has decided to walk on the sunny side of the street. It's a matter of attitude as much as anything. Decide to like what you get instead of demanding that you get what you like.

You can say to yourself, "I choose to be happy in this moment." Believe that God gives you the power to create your own happiness, and you'll discover that you have more choices than you realized. You'll learn how to create happiness for yourself and for others.

• Create happiness for others. Host a party or initiate a get-together at a favorite hangout, and enjoy the company of friends you gathered together.

#69

Be a First-Rate Version of Yourself

Your fingerprints are unique. No one else has your hands, your personality, your gifts. You are one of a kind, with something special to offer the world. Instead of comparing yourself to others and trying to live up to somebody else's image of who you should be (or what you think somebody else thinks you should be), cultivate your own unique talents and personality.

Listen to the voice of your soul. What draws you, interests you, intrigues you? What did you love to do as a child? What do you dream of becoming? Become a first-rate version of the person God created you to be.

version

> *God gives you something only you can do.*
>
> Lewis Timberlake

• Identify one talent or gift you possess that has enriched the lives of others.

#70

Adopt a Softer Tone Toward Life

The wisdom that is from above is first pure, then peaceable, gentle, willing to yield, full of mercy and good fruits, without partiality and without hypocrisy.

James 3:17 NKJV

tone

Cultivate a gentler approach to life. Be an appreciator instead of a competitor. Let the aggressive side of you take a backseat. It's not that competition is bad or that it's wrong to want to achieve great goals. But pushing too hard can be tiring for you and for those around you.

The soul enjoys a softer tone toward life. It likes to mellow down, take its time, and savor existence. A gentler attitude allows more room for the give-and-take of satisfying relationships. An open attitude creates space for God to bless and surprise you.

• Notice your driving style today. If you are an aggressive driver, slow down and let the other drivers pass you by.

#71

Expand Your Vocabulary

Words can open the windows of your mind. New words and unfamiliar concepts can expand the way you perceive the world. An unfamiliar word can add a new dimension to your thinking.

When you expand your vocabulary, you give your mind something to think about and your soul something to chew on. One delightful way to discover new words is to explore untranslatable words from other languages. For instance, the Japanese word *shibui* speaks of the kind of beauty only time can reveal. It is a reminder of the beauty of an aged face, a much-needed concept in a society that worships youthful perfection.

expand

The beginning of wisdom is this: Get wisdom, and whatever else you get, get insight.

Proverbs 4:7 NRSV

• *They Have a Word for It: A Lighthearted Lexicon of Untranslatable Words and Phrases* by Howard Rheingold offers a fun introduction to unfamiliar words. Look for it at your library or bookstore.

#72

Ignore Your Negative Thoughts

Every day the choice between good and evil is presented to us in simple ways.

William Sangster

ignore

You average 50,000 thoughts a day. Many of them will be negative: worry, fear, anger, pessimism. You can't avoid negative thoughts, but you can choose whether you'll pay attention to them or not.

Just for today, ignore your negative thoughts. When you are worried that you won't get your work finished, stop worrying and do the work. When you are angry because a driver cut you off in traffic, thank God you're safe and forget it. If you're upset about a problem, dismiss the thought and move on. Instead of giving negative thoughts power, allow the peace of God to rule your mind and soul.

• Notice your thoughts today. Are your thoughts negative or positive? Take one negative thought and turn it into a positive thought. See what happens.

#73

Read and Write Poetry

Poetry is the music of the soul. It is experience distilled into words, offering insight for the heart. Poetry can lift you beyond the daily round, reminding you of eternal perspectives. Whether you read a modern poet or an ancient psalmist, you can find expression for those nameless but deep feelings that live in your heart.

Read poetry in anthologies or explore one poet's writing. Meditate on the Psalms, the poetry of the Scriptures. Great song lyrics also offer a form of poetry to enjoy. Write your own poems and songs. Take delight in putting your feelings, experiences, and insights down.

read

> *When power narrows the areas of man's concern, poetry reminds him of the richness and diversity of his existence. When power corrupts, poetry cleanses.*
>
> John F. Kennedy

• Pick up an anthology of poems and rediscover the delights of poetry. Or listen to the poetry of lyrics to your favorite songs.

#74

Seek to Understand

> *Everyone should be quick to listen, slow to speak and slow to become angry.*
>
> James 1:19 NIV

seek

Developing intimate relationships nurtures your soul and the souls of those you become close to. If you want to cultivate deeper and more soulful relationships, put others before yourself by seeking to understand them first.

Learn to pay attention and listen. Take time to understand them before expecting them to understand you. Instead of interrupting or making value judgments, let the other person tell you how he or she feels. When you make an effort to understand another's point of view, the other person will feel understood and become more open to your point of view. Then you both feel more understood and appreciated.

• Be an active listener. Listen to what someone says and then rephrase it in your own words to make sure you understood what was said.

#75

Release Fearful Thinking

Infants have only two fears: fear of loud noises and fear of falling. All other fears are learned. Fearful thinking keeps you from doing your best, for it binds you to anxiety about the future instead of allowing you to live fully and fearlessly in the here and now.

Jesus stressed the need for faith, telling his followers to not be afraid of what was going to happen tomorrow. Today is the only day you can live, and each moment offers a choice of whether to be fearful or faithful. Release your fearful thoughts to God and claim your soul's freedom in faith.

release

God is there, ready to help; I'm fearless no matter what. Who or what can get to me?

Hebrews 13:6
THE MESSAGE

• The next time you are feeling fearful or anxious, say to yourself: "I am fine right now; God is with me in this moment."

#76

Stock Up on Colorful Candles

> *LORD, you have brought light to my life; my God, you light up my darkness.*
>
> Psalm 18:28 NLT

candles

A lit candle brings warmth and soft light to a room. Candles give a room "soul" and help create a special and welcoming atmosphere. Whether you want to encourage intimate talk over a candlelit table or create a welcoming place for worship and meditation, candles offer an easy-to-use instant transformation for any living space.

Use your imagination. Light candles when you take a fragrant herbal bath. Light a candle for your personal space for worship. Take a scented votive candle with you when you travel and make an impersonal hotel room feel more like home. Place citronella candles out on the deck for a summer party.

• Stock up on colorful candles of all shapes and sizes so that you'll be prepared for any occasion. Don't forget birthday candles for cakes!

#77

Create Your Own Fun

A soulful person creates his or her own fun. Instead of waiting for others or trying to purchase ready-made experiences, you can find inventive ways to entertain yourself and initiate shared fun.

When there isn't anyone available, enjoy solitary activities. Simple things like taking a walk, going to a movie, reading a good book, or working on a craft or project are soul-satisfying ways to entertain yourself.

When you want to be with other people, create opportunities for get-togethers. Call a friend for tea, volunteer with others, play games, or host a theme party. Use your imagination to create your own fun.

fun

> *I still find each day too short for all the thoughts I want to think, all the walks I want to take, all the books I want to read, and all the friends I want to see.*
>
> John Burroughs

• Introduce a favorite friend to your favorite walk. Bring along a snack or a picnic lunch and a Frisbee or ball for a game of catch.

#78

Take Baby Steps

> Be not afraid of growing slowly; be afraid only of standing still.
>
> Chinese Proverb

steps

Sometimes you expect yourself to make giant leaps, when what you really need to do is take small baby steps. Giant leaps make the stakes too high. Baby steps make risk-taking manageable and doable.

The next time you feel stuck or overwhelmed, see if you're raising the stakes too high and expecting giant leaps. For example, if you want to learn to ride a horse, don't expect to be jumping fences the very first day. You have to start with a walk before you can gallop.

There's more joy in living when you are gentle on yourself. Small steps can lead to greater things, letting the soul lead instead of the ego.

• Write down a cherished goal. Now break it up into simple baby steps that will take you one step at a time toward your goal.

#79

Smile at the Person in the Mirror

Go easy on yourself. Instead of looking critically at your faults, examining all your blemishes, and pointing out all your failings, learn to see yourself as a beautiful work in progress. Relax and smile at the person in the mirror.

Look at yourself through the loving and forgiving eyes of God. Smiling at yourself frees you to live life from the heart rather than from the too critical mind. It makes room for God to work with your soul, changing you from the inside out. When the soul's beauty grows, it eventually shows on the outside. You become more gentle on yourself, more loving toward others.

smile

Friendship with oneself is all-important, because without it one cannot be friends with anyone else.

Eleanor Roosevelt

• Look directly into the mirror and say aloud to yourself: "I love you, and God loves you too."

play

101 ways to give

escape

give

splurge

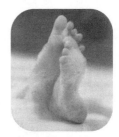

decide

your soul a lift

become

cultivate

allow

#80

Be Willing to Change

Lord, when we are wrong, make us willing to change. And when we are right, make us easy to live with.

Peter Marshall

change

Flexibility helps you create a more soulful life. Because you are open to different options, you enjoy more choices. Instead of locking yourself into rigid opinions and set ways, free yourself to explore possibilities and become more creative in your choices. Your openness and flexibility will make it easier for your soul to grow in the midst of the inevitable changes life brings.

Your willingness to change—whether your opinion or your way of doing things—will help your spiritual growth as well. When God wants to do something new in your life, he doesn't have to overcome your resistance and is able to guide you more easily.

• Take one pet opinion (such as, "All politicians are crooked") and open your mind to another possibility (such as, "Most politicians want to serve others").

#81

Express Gratitude

When someone offers you a service or does something nice for you, express your thanks. Instead of taking it for granted that people know you are appreciative, offer gratitude in words. Doing this not only honors the person who helped you, but it also focuses on the good you have received and the gifts given.

Living in an atmosphere of gratitude lifts your spirits. You become aware that you have been given much and that others have enriched your life immeasurably. Do this with God as well. Express your gratitude for the life he has given you and the blessings you have enjoyed.

gratitude

Praise the LORD! He is good. God's love never fails.

Psalm 136:1 CEV

• Write a letter of thanks to a teacher, coach, or mentor who helped you. Tell how his or her influence made you a better person.

#82

Cultivate Meaningful Relationships

> *You use steel to sharpen steel, and one friend sharpens another.*
>
> Proverbs 27:17
> THE MESSAGE

cultivate

A large circle of friends and acquaintances is wonderful. Your most important friends, however, are the ones with whom you share a deep, soulful relationship. You trust these friends with your secrets. They're the ones who have weathered the storms of life with you and trusted you with their dreams, hopes, and sorrows.

Cultivate these meaningful relationships. Get together on a regular basis, or communicate via e-mail or phone if these friends live in another part of the country. A friend who can enjoy deep conversations on the meaning of life and then share a good laugh over a bad joke is a friend worth cultivating.

• Spend a weekend away with a close friend. Stay at a bed-and-breakfast and spend time talking about what's important to both of you.

#83

Be Open to Surprises

You never know what a day will bring forth. You might receive good news in the mail. You might read a heart-stopping headline that turns your world upside down. You might get a call from a friend inviting you to a party. You might have a call from a family member about an emergency.

Life is unpredictable. Be open to surprises, for they can be the catalyst for your soul's growth. Good or bad, each experience offers lessons to be learned. Your openness makes it easier for God to work in your life. Have faith that surprises are opportunities for God to do something extraordinary for you.

surprise

Accept surprises that upset your plans, shatter your dreams, give a completely different turn to your day, and who knows? — to your life. Leave the Father free himself to weave the pattern of your days.

Dom Helder Camara

• Take a walk in unfamiliar territory—a different neighborhood, street, or park—and look for surprises and interesting sights.

#84

Discover the Pleasure of Herbs and Spices

My lover has gone down to his garden, to the beds of spices, to browse in the gardens and to gather lilies.

Song of Songs 6:2
NIV

herbs

The pungent scent of fresh basil, the spicy aroma of cinnamon, and the lush perfume of orange-flower water are only a few of the thousands of scents and flavors available on the market today. Discovering the many varieties of plants and essences is a soulful pleasure for any adventurous eater.

Explore herbs and spices, and buy a cookbook that offers creative ways to use them. Plant herbs in your garden and take delight in the scent and flavor of God's delicious creation. By expanding your culinary repertoire, you enhance the spiritual at the same time you enrich the physical.

• Go to the spice section in the grocery store or to a specialty herb and spice shop. Choose one new herb or spice to try at home.

#85

Be a Co-Creator with God

The biblical story of creation says that God created humanity in his own image. The Creator of heaven and earth made people to be creative. It is your birthright and your heritage to be a creator. You nurture your soul when you create.

Ask God to be your partner in creation. Seek the balance between taking the initiative and letting God guide you. Let God inspire your creativity—whether you are throwing a pot on a potter's wheel, making a beautiful home, building a business, or raising a child. When you create with God as your partner, you do good work.

co-creator

We are His workmanship, created in Christ Jesus for good works, which God prepared beforehand that we should walk in them.

Ephesians 2:10
NKJV

• Write a prayer affirming that you and God are partners. Make a copy to keep in sight near your work area.

#86

Relax and Let Yourself Just Be

> *Why not be oneself? That is the whole secret of a successful appearance. If one is a greyhound, why try to look like a Pekingese?*
>
> Dame Edith Sitwell

relax

Do you like loud colors and flashy clothing? Or are you more buttoned-down and conservative? Do you have a taste for the exotic or a penchant for the prim and proper? Are you athletic and sporty, funny and artistic, or down-to-earth and practical? Different people have different ways of being and expressing themselves.

A soulful person is comfortable in his or her own skin. Relax with who you are, a unique person who is loved by the God who created you. You'll find inspiration and creative joy in being yourself. When you enjoy being yourself, others will enjoy being with you.

• Take a look at what's in your closet. Give away anything that is too tight, too loose, or no longer suits your activities.

#87

Make a Pot of Soup

Making soup is a comforting and soulful thing to do. Chopping vegetables, simmering broth, adding herbs, and garnishing are satisfying, and the finished dish offers delights of taste, scent, texture, and sight. When you make soup, you are transforming simple vegetables and broth into an ambrosial and sustaining meal that feeds the body and nourishes the soul.

Make a hearty stew in winter that will stick to your ribs on a cold day. Try a refreshing cold fruit soup on a sticky summer day. Make a big pot of soup and freeze portions in individual containers. The simple delights of homemade soup will gladden your spirit.

soup

Whatever you eat or drink or whatever you do, you must do all for the glory of God.

1 Corinthians 10:31
NLT

• Make a big pot of your favorite soup and put some of it in jars to give to friends. Attach the recipe with a colorful ribbon.

#88

Meditate as You Do Mundane Tasks

Prayer and psalmody every hour is suitable, that while one's hands are busy with their tasks we may praise God with the tongue, or, if not, with the heart.

Saint Basil

meditate

God is found not only in the exalted and magnificent, but he is also at home in the humble and mundane aspects of life. Since God is always present and with you in everything you do, choose to be aware and mindful of his presence at all times.

Use everyday chores as an opportunity to commune with God and think about the things of the spirit. See washing the dishes, doing the laundry, and making beds as little services you are doing for God as well as for others. Meditate as you do mundane tasks, and discover the light of heaven in the things of earth.

• Meditate on what God is doing in your life as you weed the garden, vacuum the house, or wash the car. Sing praises and offer thanks.

#89

Appreciate Beauty

The curve of a beloved's cheek. Tall grasses bending gently in the wind. A magnificent mountain view that fills your soul with awe. A lovely woman in a beautiful dress. An exquisite work of art. Beauty waits around every corner and reveals itself around every bend in the road.

Appreciate beauty and feast your soul on its abundance. When you develop an appreciation for beauty, you nurture your soul and remind yourself that the world is full of beauty and grace. Learning to look past ugliness and uncovering beauty are metaphors for learning to look past earthly things to discover the face of God.

beauty

> *Beauty may be said to be God's trademark in creation.*
> Henry Ward Beecher

• Appreciate the beauty in others. Share with a friend or loved one a specific physical attribute or spiritual quality you admire in them.

#90

Dream by the Fire

What makes a fire so pleasant is, I think, that it is a live thing in a dead room.

Sydney Smith

dream

Dusk is settling in, and the evening lights are coming on. The hearthside glows with the warmth of the fire, and you are comfortably ensconced in an armchair or cushioned by soft pillows. It is a time for dreaming and allowing the cares of the day to fall away. The soul basks in the firelight while the imagination soars.

Let yourself dream by the fire. Build a warm fire on a winter evening. If you don't have a fireplace, create a cozy atmosphere with low lamplight, candles, and comfortable cushions. Provide a restful time and place to meditate on life, soothe your soul, and pray.

• Enjoy a fire when you go camping. Invite other campers over to roast marshmallows.

#91

Be Rooted in the Spirit

Like a mighty tree with a deep tap-root that reaches down into the ground for nourishment, root yourself in the soil of spiritual wisdom. If your foundation is firmly built on the solid rock of God's love, you will not be moved when the storms of life bluster and blow.

Be rooted in the Spirit by putting your trust in God and spending time nurturing the life of the soul. As you practice spiritual disciplines of prayer, devotional reading, meditation, and worship, you'll send roots of faith deep. When times of trouble come, you'll be prepared. You will have lifted up your soul by sinking your roots in God's love.

rooted

They are like trees planted along the riverbank, bearing fruit each season without fail. Their leaves never wither, and in all they do, they prosper.

Psalm 1:3 NLT

• Set aside a regular time for reading that nurtures your soul. Choose inspirational literature that helps set a positive tone for your day.

#92

Get Your Hands Dirty

Such is life. It is no cleaner than a kitchen; it reeks of a kitchen; and if you mean to cook your dinner, you must expect to soil your hands.

Honoré de Balzac

dirty

If you want to plant a garden, cook a meal, build a fence, or fix a car, you must get your hands dirty. It is soul satisfying to have contact with the earthly realities of soil and wood and seed. The mechanic who loves fixing a car doesn't mind the grease. A gardener who loves planting doesn't mind the good earth. They plunge in and do what they love with enthusiasm, never minding the grease or dirt.

Plunge into something you love with all your heart. Get your hands dirty and immerse yourself in the pleasure of connecting with earthy things.

• Buy a good hand-cleaner, wear some old clothes, and freely enjoy getting your hands dirty doing something you love.

#93

Pick Wildflowers

Queen Anne's lace grows wild by the side of the road. Sweet-scented honeysuckle vines entwine in the woods, and fragrant wild roses take over the riverbank. The blues and pinks of spring give way to reds and yellows of late summer and fall, offering a display of color all season long. A meadow of wildflowers can be breathtaking, a glorious reminder of the God who created all wild things.

Enjoy wildflower displays with camera and paintbrush. Feast your soul on wildflower beauties in natural areas and national parks. Learn about wildflowers that grow in your region and enjoy their seasonal beauty.

pick

> *Look at the lilies and how they grow. They don't work or make their clothing, yet Solomon in all his glory was not dressed as beautifully as they are.*
> Matthew 6:28–29
> NLT

• If legal in your state, pick wildflowers from the side of the road and make a simple bouquet for your kitchen table.

#94

See the Innocence

> We will know that we are from the truth and will reassure our hearts before him whenever our hearts condemn us; for God is greater than our hearts, and he knows everything.
>
> 1 John 3:19–20 NRSV

innocence

People can act in irritating ways. Instead of letting their outward behavior grate on you, be understanding and forgiving. Look for innocence instead of evil. Your soul sees beneath surface appearances and knows that people are often more like cranky children needing naps than evildoers bent on destruction.

When the irritating or unkind behavior of others starts to bother you, look beyond their behavior and see the innocence. Realize that they are doing the best they can with what they know at the time. Trust that God cherishes the innocence and forgives the wrong in both of you. Practicing understanding can help you find peace in difficult situations.

• The next time someone irritates you, look beyond the irritating behavior to the heart's intent. Understand and forgive childish behavior.

#95

Build a Sandcastle at the Beach

Toes wiggling in the sand, sun shining on your back, and hands and mind being absorbed in building a sandcastle make a perfect day at the beach. Let your soul bask in this child-hood delight. Enjoy the wind and waves and carefree moments of play.

As your day at the beach draws to a close, sit on the sand and watch the sunset. Watch the tide wash over your sandcastle and think of all the things in your life that have been washed away along with the sands of time. Then remember that God's loving presence in your life is as vast as the ocean.

build

> *So beautiful is the still hour of the sea's withdrawal, as beautiful as the sea's return when the encroaching waves pound up the beach.*
>
> Anne Morrow Lindbergh

• Spend a day at the beach or take a family vacation to the seashore.

flex

101 ways to give

share

believe

ask

walk

your soul a lift

nurture

relax

dream

#96

Pray Silent Blessings for Others

> *May you be blessed by the LORD, the Maker of heaven and earth.*
>
> Psalm 115:15 NIV

pray

You can be a part of healing and helping the people you meet. You can choose to make your world a better place. Your silent prayer of blessing toward the people you encounter lifts your soul as it makes a difference in the lives of others. Your prayer will bless you, too.

Pray a simple silent prayer of blessing for every person you encounter today. You may not know the effect your blessing of kindness had on the salesclerk who helped you or the stranger who opened the door for you, but you can trust that God answers every prayer.

• Say grace over the food you eat today. And don't forget to bless the hands that prepared the food.

#97

Take Up Painting

You don't have to be a Picasso or a van Gogh to enjoy the soulful pleasures of painting. Anyone can pick up a paintbrush and enjoy putting paint on canvas or paper. Remember finger painting from childhood?

Painting gives you a break from the cares of life. As you paint, you train your eye to see the colors and shapes of creation. When you are painting that still life or portrait or scenery, you have to really see what you are looking at and become aware of its unique beauty. The final picture becomes an expression of your God-given creativity.

painting

One is never tired of painting, because you have to set down not what you know already, but what you have just discovered.

William Hazlitt

• Take an introductory painting class and experiment with oils, watercolors, or acrylic paints.

#98

Develop Your Own Sense of Style

> *Every human being is intended to have a character of his own; to be what no others are, and to do what no other can do.*
>
> William Ellery Channing

style

Some people seem to have a flair for living. They live with passion, zest, and panache. Their homes reflect their personalities, and so do their clothing and jewelry choices. You won't mistake them for anyone else because they have their own sense of personal style.

You'll enjoy life more when you express who you really are. It will delight you and inspire others. Give yourself permission to experiment. Be bold and daring. Have fun as you try new things. Don't worry about making mistakes. Remember that God makes each person unique. Be yourself. Express your uniqueness with soul and style.

• Shop for clothes with a friend. Try on something that feels outrageous and out of character. You might discover a new you.

#99

Redefine *Foolish* as "Creative Freedom"

"You'll think I'm crazy, but I really want to try this," you confide in a friend. Every time you take a creative risk, it feels a bit foolish and crazy. Your soul takes wing when you take a chance. Whether that chance is learning to ice-skate, auditioning for a part in a play, or competing for the top job in your department, you will learn and grow from the experience, no matter what happens.

With the soul there is no such thing as failure. There are only trying and learning. When you are expanding your boundaries, redefine words like *failure* and *foolish* as "creative freedom."

redefine

> *One can never consent to creep when one feels the impulse to soar.*
>
> Helen Keller

• Don't let old definitions limit you. Redefine phrases that keep you from growing. For example: redefine *religious nut* as "spiritually adventurous."

#100

Give a Teddy Bear to a Friend

> *A generous man will prosper; he who refreshes others will himself be refreshed.*
>
> Proverbs 11:25 NIV

give

A cuddly teddy bear can comfort in ways that no words will. A huggable reminder of childhood comforts, a teddy bear can be held next to the heart. The gift of a teddy bear offers a simple way to encourage someone and to say, "God loves you, and so do I."

If you have a friend who needs love and encouragement, consider giving him or her a teddy bear. That lovable plush friend will be a reminder that there's another friend who cares deeply about what is happening in his or her life. And it will lift your spirits as you lift someone else's spirits.

• The next time you are in a gift or toy store, check out the stuffed animals. Find the perfect teddy bear to encourage a friend—or yourself.

#101

Drink from the Heart's Secret Springs

Your life may not seem all that different from anyone else's. You go to work, take care of home and family, and live a normal life. But you have access to a hidden source of spiritual strength that makes any life more soulful.

When you spend time with God, you drink from the secret springs of the heart. He is the One who deepens your reality and enables you to see beneath the surface of everyday life. If you commit to cultivating your relationship with God, you will experience continuous growth and transformation. And you'll enjoy a taste of heaven on earth.

drink

They are like trees planted by streams of water, which yield their fruit in its season, and their leaves do not wither. In all that they do, they prosper.

Psalm 1:3 NRSV

• Set aside a special corner of your home for quiet times alone with God. Furnish it with a comfortable chair, good lighting, candles, and fresh flowers.

*Every day the choice between good and evil
is presented to us in simple ways.*

William Sangster

Praise the LORD!
He is good. God's love never fails.

Psalm 136:1 CEV